ISBN: 0-89898-330-4
Copyright © 1984 Beam Me Up Music
c/o CPP/Belwin, Inc., 15800 N.W. 48th Avenue, Miami, Florida 33014

Layout: Adriane Pirro / Editor: Audrey L. Kleiner

CARPENTERS GREATEST HITS

We've Only Just Begun

Lyric by PAUL WILLIAMS

Music by ROGER NICHOLS

1. We've On-ly Just Be - gun   to
2. Be - fore the ris - ing sun   we
3. 4. And when the eve - ning comes   we

live, _____ White lace and prom - i - ses,
fly, _____ So man - y roads to choose,
smile, _____ So much of life a - head,

We've Only Just Begun - 3 - 1

6

A kiss for luck___ and we're on our way.___
We start out walk - ing and learn to run.___
We'll find a place___ where there's room to grow.___

And yes, We've Just Be - gun.___

Shar - ing hor - i - zons that are new to us,

watch - ing the signs a - long the way. Talk - ing it ov - er just the

Rainy Days And Mondays

Lyric by PAUL WILLIAMS

Music by ROGER NICHOLS

Moderately Slow

1. Talk-in' to my-self and feel-in'
2. What I've got they used to call the
3. What I feel has come and gone be-

old, Some-times I'd like to quit
blues, No-thing is real-ly wrong,
fore, No need to talk it out,

no-thing ev-er seems to fit. Hang-in' a-round
feel-in' like I don't be-long. Walk-in' a-round
we know what it's all a-bout. Hang-in' a-round

Rainy Days And Mondays - 4 - 1

(They Long To Be)
Close To You

Words by
HAL DAVID

Music by
BURT BACHARACH

Close To You - 2 - 1

Close To You - 2 - 2

Let Me Be The One

Lyric by PAUL WILLIAMS

Music by ROGER NICHOLS

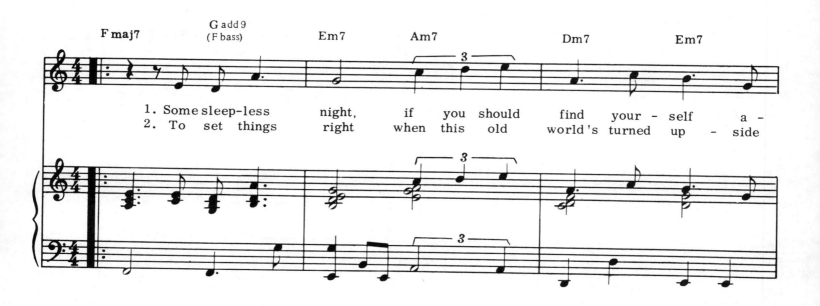

1. Some sleep-less night, if you should find your-self a-
2. To set things right when this old world's turned up-side

lone,
down,

Let me be the one___ you run to,
Let me be the one___ you run to,

Let Me Be The One - 3 - 1

Goodbye To Love

Lyrics by JOHN BETTIS

Music by RICHARD CARPENTER

Goodbye To Love - 3 - 1

18

Only Yesterday

Lyric by JOHN BETTIS

Music by RICHARD CARPENTER

Only Yesterday - 5 - 1

Only Yesterday - 5 - 2

ba - by, ba - by, feels like may - be things will be all right.

Ba - by, ba - by, your love's made me free as a song, sing-in' for - ev - er.

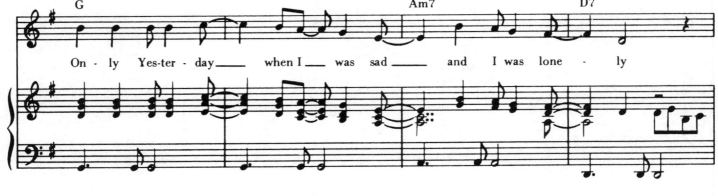

On - ly Yes-ter - day when I was sad and I was lone - ly

you showed me the way to leave the past and all it's tears be-hind me.

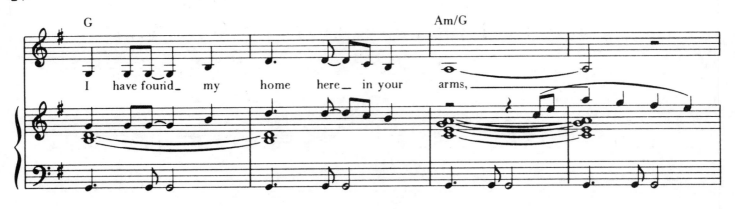

I have found my home here in your arms,

no - where else on earth I'd real - ly rath - er be.

Life waits for us share it with me, the best is a - bout to be.

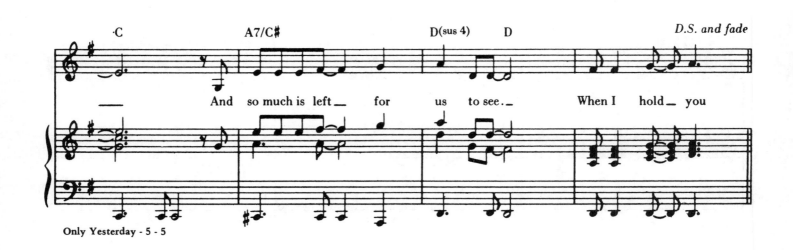

And so much is left for us to see. When I hold you

I Won't Last A Day Without You

Lyrics by PAUL WILLIAMS

Music by ROGER NICHOLS

Day af-ter day__ I must
So man-y times__ when the

face a world__of stran-gers where I don't be-long.__ I'm not that strong,
ci-ty seems__to be with-out a friend-ly face.__ a lone-ly place,

it's nice to know__ that there's some-one I __ can turn to who will
it's nice to know__ that you'll be there if__ I need you and you'll

I Won't Last A Day Without You - 5 - 1

26

I Won't Last A Day Without You - 5 - 2

I Won't Last A Day Without You - 5 - 3

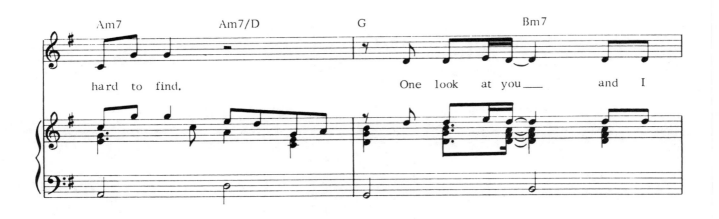

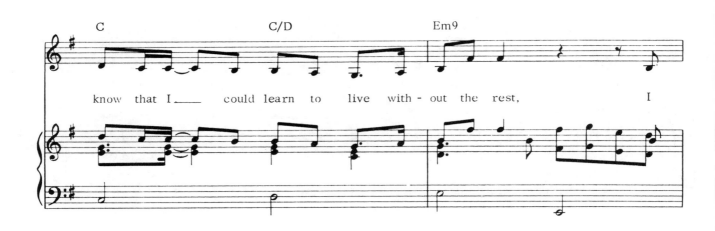

I Won't Last A Day Without You - 5 - 4

I Won't Last A Day Without You - 5 - 5

Now

Lyrics by
DEAN PITCHFORD

Music by
ROGER NICHOLS

Now - 5 - 1

fade. I was al-ways a-fraid love might for-get me,

love might let me down. Then look what I ___ found. ___

dim. poco a poco

Instrumental Solo

The

un - til   now._____

No,   I   nev- er real - ly   knew   how,   un - til

now._____

Sing

Moderately

Words and Music by
JOE RAPOSO

Sing! Sing a song. Sing out loud, sing out strong. Sing of good things, not bad;

Sing - 3 - 1

Top Of The World

Lyric by
JOHN BETTIS

Music by
RICHARD CARPENTER

Such a feel - in's com - in' ov - er me, _____ there is
Some - thing in ____ the wind has learned my name, _____ and it's

39

Top Of The World - 4 - 2

40

F#m   Em   A7   D

com-ing true e - spe-cial-ly for   me,_____   and the
day is through I hope that I will   find,_____   that to—

G   A   F#m   B7

rea - son is   clear, it's be - cause   you are   here, you're the
mor - row will be just the   same for you and   me, all I

Em7   Em7-5   A (sus4)   A

near - est thing to heav - en that I've   seen.   I'm on the
need   will be mine if you are   here.

D   G

top of the world_____ look-in' down on cre - a - tion and the

Top Of The World - 4 - 3

Top Of The World - 4 - 4

Superstar

Words and Music by
LEON RUSSELL and
BONNIE BRAMLETT

Superstar

CHORUS

Don't you re - mem - ber you told me you love me ba - by?___ You

said you'd be com - ing back___ this way___ a - gain___ may - be.___

Ba - by, ba - by, ba - by, ba - by oh,___ ba - by,___ I

love_____ you,___ I real - ly do.

1. I real - ly do.

2. I real - ly do.___

I real - ly do.___

Those Good Old Dreams

Words by JOHN BETTIS

Music by RICHARD CARPENTER

Those Good Old Dreams - 6 - 1

Those Good Old Dreams - 6 - 2

Those Good Old Dreams - 6 - 4

dark hor - i - zons,___ on - ly blue._____ It's a new___

___ day for those___ good___ old dreams._____ All my life___

___ I dreamed of lov - ing you.

2. You're a spark___

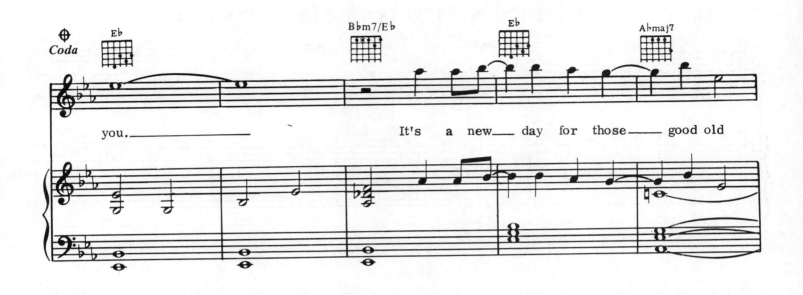

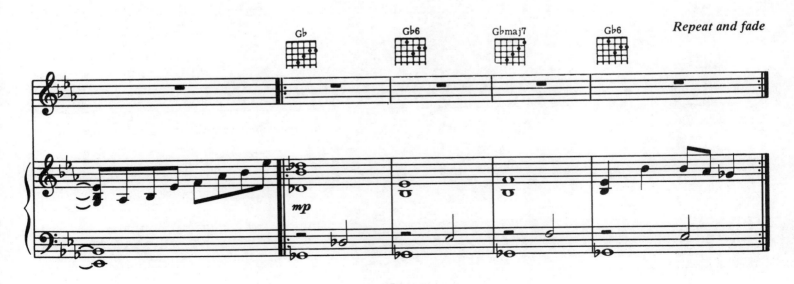

There's A Kind Of Hush

Words and Music by
LES REED and
GEOFF STEPHENS

There's A Kind Of Hush - 3 - 1

There's A Kind Of Hush - 3 - 2

Bless The Beasts And Children

Words and Music by
BARRY DE VORZON and
PERRY BOTKIN, Jr.

Bless the beasts and the chil-dren, for in this world

they have no voice, _____ they have no choice. _____

Bless the beasts and the chil-dren, for the world

can nev-er be, _____ the world they see. _____

Bless The Beasts And Children - 3 - 1

Yesterday Once More

Words and Music by
RICHARD CARPENTER and
JOHN BETTIS

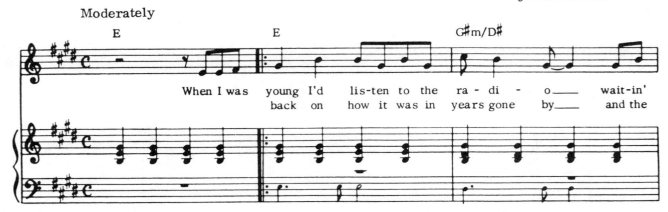

Yesterday Once More - 4 - 1

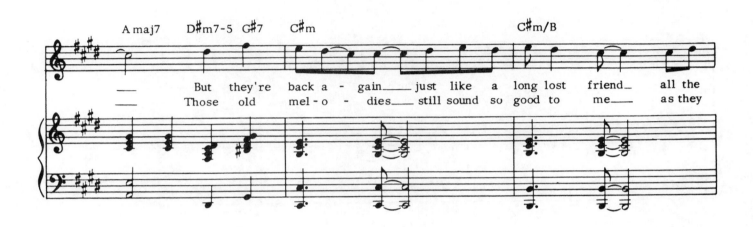

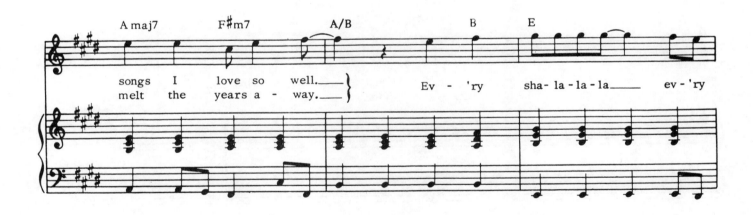

Yesterday Once More - 4 - 2

shing-a-ling-a-ling   that they're start-in' to sing___   so fine.___

when they get to the part___   where he's break-ing her heart___   it can
All my best mem-o-ries___   come back clear-ly to me___   some can

real - ly   make me cry___   just   like be - fore.___
ev - en   make me cry___   just   like be - fore.___

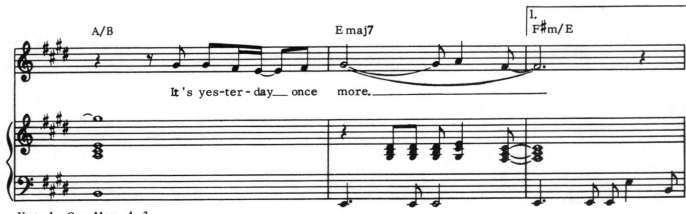

It's yes-ter-day___ once   more.___

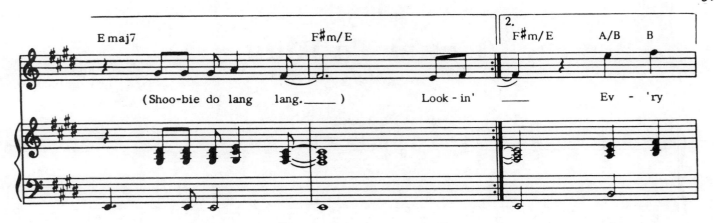

(Repeat and Fade)

Yesterday Once More - 4 - 4

Ticket To Ride

Words and Music by
JOHN LENNON and
PAUL McCARTNEY

Ticket To Ride - 2 - 1

Please Mr. Postman

Words and Music by
BRIANBERT, FREDDIE GORMAN,
GEORGIA DOBBINS and
WILLIAM GARRETT

Please Mr. Postman - 3 - 1

It's Going To Take Some Time

Words and Music by
CAROLE KING and
TONI STERN

It's gon-na take ___ some time ___ this time ___ to get my-self ___ in shape.

I real-ly fell ___ out of line ___ this time, ___ I real-ly missed ___ the gate.

The birds on the tel-e-phone line, *(next time)* are cry-in' out ___ to me, ___ *(next time)* and

It's Going To Take Some Time - 3 - 1

It's Going To Take Some Time - 3 - 3

For All We Know

Words by
ROBB WILSON and
JAMES GRIFFIN

Music by
FRED KARLIN

For All We Know - 3 - 1

70

For on-ly time _____ will ___ tell us so_____

And love may grow FOR ALL ___ WE KNOW.

(Waa _____

_____ '). Love _____ Look at the

For All We Know - 3 - 3

Make Believe It's Your First Time

Words and Music by
BOB MORRISON and
JOHNNY WILSON

Make Believe It's Your First Time - 5 - 1

72

Make Believe It's Your First Time - 5 - 2

74

Make Believe It's Your First Time - 5 - 4

Make Believe It's Your First Time - 5 - 5

CARPENTERS

All their best in collections and sheet music.

BOOKS

Complete, Volume 1
___ (P0618SMX)

Bless The Beasts And The Children ● Can't Smile Without You ● I Can Dream, Can't I ● Please Mr. Postman ● Ticket To Ride.

Complete, Volume 2
___ (P0619SMX)

Breaking Up Is Hard To Do ● For All We Know ● Goofus ● I Won't Last A Day Without You ● Rainy Days And Mondays ● Top Of The World ● We've Only Just Begun.

Greatest Hits
___ (P0593SMX)

Top Of The World ● Ticket To Ride ● Let Me Be The One ● Goodbye To Love ● For All We Know.

Voice Of The Heart
___ (P0538SMX)

Make Believe It's Your First Time ● Ordinary Fool ● Prime Time Love ● Your Baby Doesn't Love You Anymore ● Two Lives ● Sailing On The Tide.

Christmas Portrait
___ (P0673SMX)

An overture medley Ave Maria ● Christmas Song ● Christmas Waltz ● First Snowfall ● It's Christmas Time ● O Come, O Come Emmanuel ● Sleigh Ride and more popular and traditional favorites.

SHEET MUSIC

Close To You (They Long To Be)
Easy Piano/Pamela Schultz
___ (3762CP2X)

For All We Know (PS/Lewis)
___ (T5320FPV)

I Won't Last A Day Without You
___ (7466ISMX)

We've Only Just Begun
___ (1487WSMX)
___ Easy Piano/D. Coates (1487WP2X)
___ Easy Piano/J. Brimhall (1568WSP2)
___ Early Int. Piano/D.C. Glover (PA02214)

This music is available at leading music dealers in the United States and Canada.